GUIDE DOGS

BY PHYLLIS RAYBIN EMERT

EDITED BY DR. HOWARD SCHROEDER

Professor in Reading and Language Arts
Dept. of Elementary Education
Mankato State University

PRODUCED & DESIGNED BY
BAKER STREET PRODUCTIONS

CRESTWOOD HOUSE

LIBRARY OF CONGRESS CATALOGING IN PUBLICATION DATA
Emert, Phyllis Raybin.
  Guide dogs (for the blind).

  (Working dogs)
  SUMMARY: Describes the selection and training of guide dogs and how
they are paired with a blind person.
  1. Guide-dogs—Juvenile literature. (1. Guide dogs) I. Schroeder, How-
ard. II. Title. III. Series.
EV1780.S4E46   1985   636.7'0886   85-12756
ISBN 0-89686-282-8 (lib. bdg.)

International Standard Book Number:	Library of Congress Catalog Card Number:
Library Binding 0-89686-282-8	85-12756

ILLUSTRATION CREDITS

Peter R. Hornby: Cover, 4, 8, 17, 20, 24, 28, 33, 37, 41, 44
The Seeing Eye: 7, 11, 14
E. James Pitrone for the Seeing Eye: 18, 23, 30, 34, 38, 42, 43, 46

CRESTWOOD HOUSE
Hwy. 66 South, Box 3427
Mankato, MN 56002-3427

JUVENILE
636.708

Table of contents

The author would like to thank Catherine Swan and The Seeing Eye in Morristown, New Jersey, and Jennifer Bassing and Guide Dogs for the Blind in San Rafael, California, for their assistance and cooperation: Special thanks to Cammy Emert.

1.
Morris Frank and Buddy

It was a very special birthday party. Buddy was ten years old. Hundreds of people were there to help her celebrate.

"Look this way, Buddy," said one man with a camera.

Photographers took Buddy's picture. It would

Most of the first seeing eye dogs were German shepherds.

appear on the front pages of their newspapers. She had friends all across the country who liked to read about her.

The birthday cake was one of a kind. It was made from meat and biscuits. The candles were made of butter, one of Buddy's favorite foods. Everyone sang "Happy Birthday." Then they clapped loudly.

It didn't matter that there was no ice cream at this party. Ten year old Buddy was not a boy or a girl. She was a very special German shepherd dog.

Buddy was the first guide dog in America. Without Buddy, The Seeing Eye, and other guide-dog schools, could never have started.

Buddy's master was a man named Morris Frank. He was blind. With Buddy's help, Morris could go anywhere. He could do anything that a sighted person could do. But it was different before he had Buddy.

Morris became blind during a boxing match when he was sixteen years old. People act in different ways when a terrible accident happens. Some give up, thinking they can never have a happy life. They don't even try to help themselves.

But Morris never gave up. He went to college. He got a part-time job selling insurance. He tried to live a full life. But, like many blind people, he always had to ask someone to help him.

He dated girls, but his friends had to guide him around. Morris paid a man to lead him to the offices and homes of customers when he sold insurance. What Morris wanted most was the freedom to come and go as he pleased.

One night his father brought home a magazine. It was called The Saturday Evening Post.

"Sit down, Morris," said his father. "I must read you this article. It's about dogs who lead the blind. The blind person tells the dog where to go."

Morris got excited as he listened to the article. It was called "The Seeing Eye" and was written by Dorothy Harrison Eustis. It told about a school in Potsdam, Germany, that was started for men who were blinded in the War. The school trained German shepherd dogs to lead them.

"A complete change took place before my eyes," said Mrs. Eustis. "One moment there was an unsure, stumbling blind man, tapping with a cane. The next moment there was a confident person, with his dog firmly in hand and his head up."

When Mr. Frank finished reading, Morris said, "Please help me write a letter to Mrs. Eustis. I must have one of those dogs." Morris' letter asked how he could help start a school for these dogs in America. "If you train me," he promised, "I will bring back my dog and show Americans how a blind man can be on his own."

Mrs. Eustis liked Morris' letter. She called him on the telephone and asked, "Will you come to Switzerland to learn to use a guide dog?"

Morris Frank, Dorothy Harrison Eustis, and Buddy, as seen in 1936.

"I'd go anywhere for that," he answered. So, in 1928, nineteen year old Morris traveled by ship to the Eustis Kennels.

Morris' guide dog was a female German shepherd. When she licked Morris' face, he knew that they would be friends. Her name was Kiss. But Morris called her Buddy.

After weeks of training and practice, Buddy and Morris went out on their own. Morris held on to Buddy with the use of a special harness. He gave her directions by saying, "right," "left," or "forward."

German shepherds make good guide dogs because they're smart and even tempered.

Buddy sat down at curbs. When Morris gave the command, "forward," she crossed the street — but only when it was safe. For the first time since he lost his sight, Morris didn't need anyone's help.

Buddy's real test as a guide dog came when they were walking along a road one day. Suddenly, Morris heard the sound of hoofbeats. Buddy acted quickly. She pulled Morris off the road. She pulled so hard that he almost lost his balance! Morris heard horses run past them. The runaway animals were dragging a large wagon that was crashing along behind.

Because of Buddy's quick thinking, Morris was pulled from danger just in time. Buddy had saved Morris' life!

The time had come for Morris and Buddy to leave Switzerland and return to America. "Now you have to prove two things to the people in the United States," Mrs. Eustis said to Morris. "You have to walk in the big, busy cities the way sighted people do. Prove that a blind man with a guide dog can go anywhere."

"Then get everyone to accept Buddy. That means in stores and restaurants, and on buses and trains. Do these things and I'll help you start a guide-dog school in America."

When they got to the United States, Morris and Buddy went to New York City. A newspaper reporter dared them to cross West Street. It was the busiest street in the City. "Forward," said Morris. He and Buddy started across the street, followed by a group of reporters.

The reporters had never seen a blind man led by a guide dog before. It was a strange sight on such a busy and noisy street. Morris could hear the loud honks of the car horns in his ears. He felt the cars whiz past. Through it all, Buddy stayed calm. They walked very slowly, with Buddy moving and then stopping, as the traffic raced by.

"We made it, girl!" said Morris as they reached the other curb.

The reporters were amazed. One of them had taken a cab to get across the street. Some of the others had turned back. They were still standing on the other side. The next day newspapers printed stories and pictures. Soon, everyone in New York City knew about Buddy and Morris.

The two traveled from city to city to prove Buddy could guide Morris anywhere. Wherever they went, reporters wrote stories about them. Soon they were so well-known that Buddy was allowed in most stores, restaurants, and hotels.

True to her word, Mrs. Eustis helped Morris start the first guide-dog school in America. In January, 1929, it opened in Nashville, Tennessee (Morris' hometown). It was called The Seeing Eye, after the title of the article written by Mrs. Eustis. Later, the school moved to Whippany, New Jersey, and then to

Buddy safely guides Morris in busy, big-city traffic.

Morristown, New Jersey, where it is located today.

Morris and Buddy spoke about The Seeing Eye wherever they went. They met with presidents, congressmen, and other famous people.

In 1938, Buddy and Morris flew from Chicago, Illinois, to Morristown on an airplane. It was the first time a Seeing Eye dog was allowed on a regular flight. Buddy had helped get guide dogs accepted on buses, railroads, and street cars. With this airplane flight, Buddy and Morris finished what Mrs. Eustis asked of them. Guide dogs were now accepted everywhere.

Buddy died at the age of 12½ years. Letters praising her came from all over the world. She was buried with her harness and leash on the grounds of The Seeing Eye.

"I owe Buddy more than I can ever tell," Morris said. "She gave me courage to do things that I never would have tried had she not come into my life."

Since that time Morris has had other dogs. All were named Buddy. There are many other guide dogs now, too. They have names like Abby, Lancer, Crystal, Barry, and Katie. But no other Seeing Eye dog, except Morris Franks', is allowed the special name of Buddy.

2.

Guide dogs in history

For hundreds of years dogs have been used to guide blind people.

In a Chinese scroll from the thirteenth century, there's a dog guiding his blind master. Even great artists like Rembrandt, Tintoretto, and Gainsborough have painted blind men with their dogs. But all the dogs were trained by their own blind masters.

In 1819, a Viennese priest, Father Johann Klein, suggested that dogs for the blind should be trained by people who could see. However, training guide dogs didn't begin until 1916, in Germany. The dogs were trained to guide blind soldiers.

American organizations for the blind knew about the German work with guide dogs. But they felt that German shepherds were too vicious.

The 1927, magazine article by Dorothy Eustis created a wave of interest among Americans. After Morris Frank (and Buddy) helped start The Seeing Eye other guide-dog schools were organized.

In 1939, Leader Dogs for the Blind opened its doors in Michigan. Then in 1942, Guide Dogs for the Blind was started in California. Today, there are eleven guide-dog programs in the United States.

Morris Frank and Buddy convinced Americans that German shepherds were not vicious.

3.
Special qualities

To lead the blind, a dog must be alert, dependable, and intelligent. Although many breeds have these qualities, they still don't make good guide dogs.

Some dogs would instantly obey a command, even if it risked the life of its master. The guide dog has to think for itself. It must try to follow instructions. It must also keep its master safe from harm. The guide dog must have the "ability to disobey."

Guide dogs should be strong enough to pull their masters out of danger. They shouldn't be so strong that they knock them off their feet. The dog must be of medium size — just tall enough for its master to reach the special harness it wears.

A guide dog's coat must withstand all kinds of weather. The outercoat should be easily bathed and groomed. Since the dogs walk long distances, they must have strong legs and feet. They shouldn't be too shy. They must not be easily frightened of crowds and noises.

Different types of dogs, who have these qualities, have been trained to guide the blind. However, most guide dogs today belong to one of three breeds: the German shepherd, the Labrador retriever, or the golden retriever.

German shepherds

Long ago, dogs were trained to herd and protect flocks of cattle and sheep. These herding dogs were called shepherds. They were very smart. They did their jobs well. They were tough and healthy.

In 1889, Captain Max Von Stephanitz, became interested in making the shepherd dog even better. He was later called the father of the German shepherd breed. To Von Stephanitz, a German, the dog only had value if it was intelligent, strong, and had an even temper. It had to be a good-working partner. In Germany, breeders began to stress these important points over a dog having good looks. They produced high-quality shepherd dogs. The grandsons and granddaughters of these dogs now live all over the world. They are known as German shepherds.

Females are twenty-two to twenty-four inches tall (56.4 - 61.5 cm) at the shoulder. They weigh between sixty and seventy pounds (27.3 - 31.8 kg). Male dogs are twenty-four to twenty-six inches (61.5 - 66.6 cm) at the shoulder and weigh seventy-five to eighty-five pounds (34.1 - 38.6 kg).

A shepherd's thick undercoat protects the dog from cold and insects. The outercoat is short, straight, wiry, and resists rain.

The German shepherd dog comes in many colors.

They're brown, tan, black, or gray. Some are streaked or spotted with a darker color. A few are solid white.

This is common coloring for a German shepherd.

The Labrador retriever is usually very gentle and smart.

Labrador retrievers

For hundreds of years, dogs have helped people hunt. Retrieving dogs are trained to recover game that has been shot. The dogs watch where birds, or small animals, fall. On command, they bring the game back to their masters.

The Labrador retriever has excellent scenting powers, and is very smart. Labradors have "soft mouths" — they're careful not to bite or rip the game they are carrying in their mouths. Labradors are also kind and outgoing. They're almost always willing to please their masters.

The Labrador retriever is a solidly-built, medium-sized dog. Males are 22½ to 24½ inches (57.7 - 62.8 cm) tall at the shoulder. Females are 21½ to 23½ inches (55.1 - 60.3 cm) tall. They weigh between fifty-five and seventy-five pounds (25 - 34.1 kg). Males are usually heavier than females.

The Labrador's coat is short, straight, and very thick. It feels rough to the touch. Water runs freely off the Labrador's coat, which protects it from the cold.

Labradors come in black, chocolate, or yellow colors. The yellow dogs range from a fox-red to a cream color.

Golden retrievers

The golden retriever is one of the most popular dogs in the world. They are beautiful, smart, and even tempered. Goldens were first bred to recover hunters game in the water or on land. Like Labradors and other retrievers, they have soft mouths. Goldens also make good house pets.

Muscular and strong, golden retrievers come in many shades. Most are a rich-gold color. But some are now bred to be a creamy white. Others are a deep-red color.

Males are twenty-three to twenty-four inches (58.9 - 61.5 cm) tall at the shoulder. They weigh sixty-five to seventy-five pounds (29.5 - 34 kg). Females are 21½ to 22½ inches tall (55.1 - 57.6 cm) and weigh sixty to seventy pounds (27.2 - 31.8 kg).

Their coats are thick, soft and water resistant. A heavy undercoat protects them from the cold. The golden retriever has fringes of hair, called "feathering," on the back of their front legs. Heavier feathering may also be found on the neck, under the tail, and on the backs of the thighs.

A Golden retriever.

4.

There are eleven guide-dog schools in the United States today. Their goals are the same. They all train dogs to guide the blind. However, each program may differ in the way the dogs are taught. Some schools use staff members for early training, while others use volunteers. Therefore, what follows is only a general description of training guide dogs.

Puppies

Many guide-dog schools breed their own puppies. Some are kept for the breeding program. The others go into the training program. Puppies not chosen for either program are given away. The schools make sure that these puppies get good homes in the community.

At The Seeing Eye in New Jersey, information about how the puppies look and act goes into a computer. The computer helps the staff match the dogs later for breeding.

Volunteers

At Guide Dogs for the Blind in California, volunteers weigh and measure the puppies when they're a few weeks old. Their hearing and eyes are also tested. The volunteers write down whether the puppy is alert, curious, or shy.

In one test, a volunteer suddenly jumps at the dog to see how scared it gets. In another, the puppies walk across floors of wire mesh, metal, and gravel to see how they act.

Other tests include going up and down stairs, walking near a bicycle, and fetching. Most puppies finish the tests well and go on to the next step in their training.

Home placement

At the age of two or three months, most guide-dog programs place the puppies in the homes of volunteer families. Families with 4-H Club members are often used. The 4-H Club is for children nine to nineteen years of age. Members take part in projects which help them "learn by doing." Raising a guide-dog puppy is one of many 4-H activities. The 4-H member is put in charge of the puppy. The rest of the family helps raise the puppy.

The pup must sleep beside their young master's bed at night. It is in the house as much as possible. The pup is taken for walks on busy streets. The pup goes to stores and restaurants. It goes on buses, up

Seeing eye dogs are trained as puppies to stay with their masters at all times.

23

A guide dog in training goes everywhere with members of volunteer families.

and down stairs and elevators, on trains, and in cars. The puppy wears a special green coat. Words on the coat say that it's a guide-dog puppy in training.

The pup is taught to love people and enjoy family life. The 4-H member takes the pup to 4-H meetings. There the pup learns to "sit," "come," "stay," "down," and "fetch." There are 4-H Field Days every three months. At the Field Day, guide-dog puppies and their young handlers compete for ribbons.

Hundreds of 4-H members and their puppies take part in the Annual Field Day at Guide Dogs for the Blind. The youngest puppies go through a special obstacle course for guide dogs. The handlers try to get the puppies through the course without being distracted. Unusual objects are placed on the course. The pups walk past a loud cement mixer and a working steam engine. They also have to pass other strange and noisy objects.

The 4-H member writes down the puppy's progress. Staff members from the school check on the puppies to make sure things are going smoothly. All these things will help the pup later when it begins real guide-dog training.

When the dogs are between eleven and eighteen-months-old, they are returned to the guide-dog school. (The age of return is different for each school). This is the hardest part of the guide-dog project. The young people must say goodbye to their pet. Often there are tears. But these boys and girls feel proud. They have helped the puppy on its way to becoming a guide dog.

The 4-H members and volunteer families often train several puppies. The Seeing Eye's "Buddy Award" was given to Evelyn Henderson in 1978. She raised more than two hundred puppies for The Seeing Eye over twenty-seven years.

When the pups return to the school kennels, they are assigned to instructors. They now face a three to five month training period to become a guide dog.

Beginning training

At the beginning of training the dog must learn that it's good to please its master. The dog gets a pat on the head for a good job. The instructor says, "good girl (or boy)." When the dog makes a mistake, the instructor says loudly "no" or "phui" (fwee) and jerks on the leash. ("Phui" is a Swiss word for "bad" used at The Seeing Eye. "No" is used at Guide Dogs for the Blind and most other schools.)

By repeating the same things, the dog will soon learn what is expected. Praise, and the instructor's happiness, is the dog's reward for doing well.

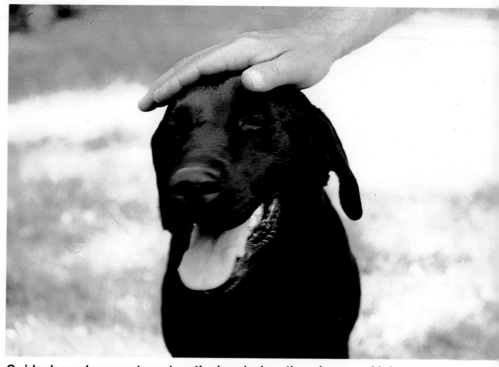

Guide dogs always get a pat on the head when they do a good job.

Obedience

First, the dog is taught to "come" properly. It must run to the instructor's side instantly and sit, no matter where it is or what it's doing. Next comes the basic obedience commands like "sit," "lie down," or "fetch." Since volunteer families have worked on obedience, most dogs will easily pass this part of the training.

Harnesses and curbs

The dog must then learn to work in a harness. The harness handle is a stiff, U-shaped bar which will be held by the blind person. It is attached to the dog by a chest and stomach strap. The dogs are trained to pull forward in their harnesses. They must walk on the left side, and a bit ahead of the instructor who acts as the blind master.

An important lesson for the dog to learn is stopping and sitting at curbs. Otherwise, the blind person could fall off the curb. The curb also lets a blind person know they are at the end of a block. They can follow directions by counting blocks. When a guide dog stops at the curb, the master either gives the signal "right," "left," or "forward." The dog learns to obey only when it is safe.

If the dog doesn't stop at a curb, the instructor will pretend to trip off the curb. He then taps the curb with a foot and loudly says "phui" or "no" to the dog. The dog knows something is wrong. Then the instructor steps back on the sidewalk and calls "come." The dog walks over and sits on the instructor's left side. It is rewarded with a "good girl (or boy)."

The instructor then says "forward." If the dog does not pause at the curb, the instructor trips again. Then comes another tap and a loud "phui" or "no."

In the second week of training, the dog is introduced to the harness.

The instructor steps back onto the sidewalk again and says "come." Then "good girl (or boy)" is said when the dog sits at the instructor's side. This is done again and again until the dog learns to stop at the curb.

Soon the dog starts to understand that the curb is dangerous. As it comes close to the next one, it might slow down. The instructor says "hup up" (a Swiss term used at The Seeing Eye) or "hop up" (used at Guide Dogs for the Blind). It means "go on, keep going." If the dog stops and sits at the curb, it is praised. If it doesn't stop, the instructor repeats the process.

Doing the same thing many times the same way is the most important part of guide-dog training. Each and every time the dog obeys, it is praised. All corrections must be made instantly.

The instructors have to judge each dog's temperament. They differ from one another, just like people. A "soft dog" is one which is upset by corrections. It needs more praise. A "hard dog" may not obey the instructor. This dog needs firm corrections.

Other dangers

The dog is now taught to lead its master around things that may block the way. The instructor pretends to walk into a tree and trips. The tree is slapped. "Phui" or "no" is said. The dog knows something is wrong. The instructor says, "Come," and the dog is praised for obeying. They try it again. After a time, the dog learns the tree is dangerous and leads the instructor around it.

The dog must be taught that moving cars are dangerous. One of the other instructors drives a car slowly along the street. The instructor and dog walk "forward" across the street. The instructor pretends to walk into the car as it passes. The instructor slaps the car and says "phui" or "no."

The dog knows something is wrong. Then the instructor says, "Come." The dog is praised when it sits at the instructor's side. The exercise is repeated many times. Soon the dog stops to let the car go by. It starts to understand that the car is dangerous. Then it guides the instructor safely across the street.

The same kind of training is used for things that could hit the blind person's head. These could be low-hanging signs, awnings, or branches of trees or bushes. The dog must be aware of things it can pass under, but its master cannot. With practice, the dog will learn to lead its master around these dangers.

Soon the walks with the instructor get harder. Instead of a quiet street with houses, they go to a busy street. The dog learns to guide the instructor in heavy traffic. It learns to go in and out of buildings. Each dog must also learn to disobey a command if it

Each dog must learn to think on its own.

could bring harm to its master. A dog that can't make these safety decisions is cut from the program.

The dog is given a final test at the end of the training period. The dog guides the instructor who wears a blindfold. During this final test, the director of the school follows the dog and the instructor. The director decides whether the dog is ready to be placed with a blind person.

This instructor gives one of her dogs the final blindfold test in Morristown, New Jersey.

The blind student

First-time students spend about four weeks living at the school with their new guide dog. People replacing their old dogs may finish this training in a shorter time.

At Guide Dogs for the Blind, the student first learns the commands needed to work with their dog. They're also taught how to care for the dog and how to use the harness.

At The Seeing Eye, new students go on a walk with a guide dog and an instructor soon after they arrive. The student is taught the different commands and how to correct the dog. By the end of the walk, the instructor knows the student's strong and weak points. The instructor notes the student's walking speed and personality-type. These things are later used to help match the student with the right guide dog.

Instructors try to match the size and temperament of the dog with the blind person's needs. A small, friendly woman might be best with a small, softer-type dog. A very nervous person might need a calm, steady dog.

Once the student gets a dog, they live together twenty-four hours a day. The dog sleeps beside the student's bed. The student feeds, brushes, and plays with the dog all the time. The dog soon understands that this new person cares for it very much. It begins to accept the blind student as its new master.

Training starts with obedience practice. The dog learns to respond to the student, and not to the instructor. After a short time, training takes place on the streets. The instructor follows close behind. The student must learn to walk at a fast pace and stand up straight. The instructor reminds the student to praise the dog, or to walk faster or slower. After a while, the instructor only follows at a distance.

Working as a team

It is out on the streets that the dog and student learn to work as a team. The dog can see the dangers. But the master must direct the dog. The student must also keep track of the number of blocks and where to turn.

At a street corner, the student listens for the traffic to stop. Then the "forward" signal is given. The dog obeys only if it is safe. Anything dropped by its master is retrieved by the guide dog. The dog will ignore other animals and people. (By the way, a dog wearing a harness is "on duty," and should never be petted by other people.)

Some students live in busy cities. Their training will take place on city streets. Other students live on farms or in small towns. Most of their training will be on country roads and in nearby villages. Each school tries to meet the different needs of each student.

The blind person must learn to trust the dog's judgement. When that trust is given, the dog will try to please its master. The guide dog will keep its master safe from harm.

A guide dog crosses a street only when it is safe to do so.

Graduation and home

At the end of the training period, graduation ceremonies are held at most guide dog schools. Blind students and their dogs take part. Members of the student's family may also attend.

A blind person enjoys his new freedom.

Often 4-H members, or other volunteer families who have raised a guide-dog puppy, will be at that dog's graduation. At some schools, ceremonies are open to the public.

After graduation, the blind person returns home with the guide dog. Some blind people travel with family members. Others go alone with their dogs, enjoying their new freedom.

The student and the dog must adjust to daily life together at home. When out of the harness, the dog is like every other family pet. However, the blind person feeds and cares for the dog. This way, the dog always knows that the blind person is its master.

Many schools send instructors on visits to the homes of students. Others send instructors only if there are problems. All schools keep in touch by telephone or letter.

If it stays healthy, the average guide dog works eight to twelve years. If the dog gets too old or has a health problem, the blind person gets a new dog. Some programs let the blind person keep the old dog as a pet. Other programs feel the old dog will have problems getting along with the new dog. Then the school finds a good home for the old dog. Some blind people have had as many as six or eight guide dogs in their lives.

5.

Training instructors

The success of today's guide-dog programs depends on the quality of the instructors. They must be smart. Instructors must also be strong. They may walk ten miles each day while training the dogs.

It often takes three months to train a dog to guide a blind person. But it takes years to train an instructor to teach the dogs. California is the only state which requires that instructors be licensed.

Each apprentice instructor lives, blindfolded, with a class at the school for ten days. They share a room with a blind student and are assigned a guide dog. In this way, the apprentice instructors will get to know how the student feels. The apprentice helps licensed instructors in the care and training of guide dogs. Later, they help with the teaching of blind students.

Finally, they must pass a two-part exam given by the California State Guide Dog Board of Examiners. In the first part, the questions are answered orally. The second part is a blindfold test in city traffic, with a guide dog the apprentice has trained.

Guide-dog schools outside of California have similar apprentice programs. Those states just don't license the instructors.

Apprentice instructors help licensed instructors to train guide dogs.

This seeing eye apprentice is showing a guide dog low branches, which the dog must learn to avoid.

Who gets a guide dog?

Not every blind person can have a guide dog. Many schools feel that people under the age of sixteen are not mature enough to handle a guide dog. Some programs have an upper-age limit. That's because the dogs need to be walked by their masters two to three miles a day. Adults over the age of fifty-five, getting their **first** guide dog, may not be able to do that much walking.

Some blind people don't like dogs. Others feel that it's too much trouble to care for a dog. A guide dog can help only if the blind person wants to get around by themselves.

Like any other dog, a guide dog needs a great deal of attention.

Many blind people prefer to use a cane.

There are also many blind people that don't feel a need to have a guide dog. They feel that they get around just as well by using a cane.

The Cost

Blind students pay The Seeing Eye $150.00 for their guide dogs. The $150.00 also covers the student's training at the school and follow-up visits by instructors. Replacement dogs and training cost

$50.00. The student's travel costs to and from the school are paid by The Seeing Eye.

No one is ever turned away if they don't have enough money to pay for a dog and training. The Seeing Eye helps each student decide their own payment schedule. Some pay a small amount each month, even if it's as little as one dollar.

At Guide Dogs for the Blind, there is no charge to the blind person for the dog, training, or replacement dogs. However, travel costs to-and-from the school are paid by the student. Other guide-dog schools have similar charges.

It's very expensive to run a guide-dog school. It costs about $10,000 to fully train one blind person and one guide dog. Most of the schools are supported by gifts of money. The money is donated by people, businesses, and groups. Some groups sponsor fund-raising events and give the money to the guide-dog schools.

An Important Job

Today, thousands of guide-dogs across the country do the job they were trained to do. These animals lead blind men and women out into the world. The dogs give blind people freedom, confidence, and self-respect. For many blind people, these dogs have made life worth living.

Guide dogs have given blind people the freedom to go almost anywhere.

Glossary

ABILITY TO DISOBEY — *A guide dog will not follow instructions if its master is put in danger by doing so.*

APPRENTICE INSTRUCTOR — *A beginning instructor, who learns by helping and watching licensed instructors.*

BUDDY — *The first guide dog in America — a female German shepherd.*

FEATHERING — *Fringes of hair along the tail and legs of certain dogs.*

4-H — *Clubs for young people nine to nineteen years of age. Members take part in projects such as raising a guide dog puppy.*

HARD DOG — *Dog which may not obey; needs firm corrections.*

HARNESS — *The U-shaped bar held by a blind person. It's attached to the guide dog by a chest and stomach strap.*

HUP UP, HOP UP — *Means "go on" or "keep going."*

PHUI — *Swiss word for "bad" which is used at The Seeing Eye (pronounced fwee).*

SOFT DOG — *A gentle dog which is upset by corrections, needs praise.*

SOFT MOUTH — *Dog which don't bite or rip at game they are bringing back to their masters.*

TEMPERAMENT — *The emotional characteristics that are special to each dog; its personality or frame of mind.*

THE SEEING EYE — *The first guide dog school in America; located in Morristown, New Jersey.*

47

READ ABOUT THE MANY KINDS OF DOGS THAT WORK FOR A LIVING:

HEARING-EAR DOGS

GUIDE DOGS

WATCH/GUARD DOGS

LAW ENFORCEMENT DOGS

SEARCH & RESCUE DOGS

STUNT DOGS

SLED DOGS

MILITARY DOGS

CRESTWOOD HOUSE